Me'nino's Tail

Me'nino's Tail

A Cat's Story

Renee M. Costello-Hager

authorHOUSE®

AuthorHouse™
1663 Liberty Drive
Bloomington, IN 47403
www.authorhouse.com
Phone: 1-800-839-8640

Published by AuthorHouse   12/19/2012

ISBN: 978-1-4817-0081-8 (sc)
ISBN: 978-1-4817-0079-5 (e)

Library of Congress Control Number: 2012923821

Photos: *Me'nino, taken by Ronald J. Costello*

Cover Drawing: *Me'nino & Mom, by Ronald J. Costello*

Dedicated to my loving parents,
Louisa** and **Ronald Costello,
who could not be more appreciated
for the sacrifices they made to give me
a wonderful childhood.

Contents

Prologue

December 2010 was the month we received the worst news we would ever want to hear: your mother has Stage-4 lung cancer. She wasn't even a smoker. My father and I started our year-long journey with mom's illness in January 2011.

I visited my parents monthly, sometimes more frequently, throughout that year to attend meetings with her oncologist. Things were going well and we thought we had the cancer under control. Unfortunately, in August of 2011, our hopes were shattered. We were told that the tumors were still growing and different chemo treatments needed to begin that month. This appointment was running late, and my father had to leave before he heard this news. This was the only appointment my father ever missed and telling him was going to be difficult.

He was going to need a distraction. So, later that month, my mother and I decided that my father needed something else to focus on rather than her illness. We thought: what would bring him joy and make him smile again? A kitten. It's been years since they had a cat and they always talked about getting another one. Now was the time. So, one Saturday afternoon, my mother and I went to the local animal shelter and adopted one special little kitten.

This is his story.

Homeward Bound . . .

Homeward Bound . . .

My name is Me'nino and this is my story. You will learn more about my name later.

I don't remember much before I ended up in a shelter, but I think someone found me wandering around lost and confused and brought me to this place where they have so many more cats and kittens—and, oh my, DOGS! Thank goodness they kept all of us kitties in a separate area. I don't know if I could handle being around all those loud barking dogs. I was quite young, probably about three or four months old at the time. I spent the majority of my young life in a small cage all by myself in this shelter. I'm not complaining, mind you; I was happy, well fed, played with, and well taken care of.

I remember this one summer day, I'm thinking probably August, because it was very hot. These two lovely ladies came in; a mother and daughter, I presumed. I heard them talking to my keeper but didn't really understand what was going on. All I know is I liked these women and I wanted to get to know them. As they moved closer to my cage, I knew I needed to get their attention, so I stuck my tiny paws through the slats of my cage in a very playful manner.

Finally, the daughter asked my keeper if she could take me out and hold me. She said yes. So the daughter opened my cage and took me out. I did not resist like I have seen some of the other kitties here do. Well, I thought, I have to win these two ladies over, so I turned on all my cute charms. I purred and purred and purred some more. I was so loud that I made her smile and laugh. Then she handed me off to her mother. And I loved this lady right from the start, because I could sense there was something terribly wrong with her. She was ill, I thought. I knew then that I really needed to be with this family. They needed me as much as I needed them. You see, we cats can sense when something isn't quite right. Well, I just couldn't get enough of

this woman. I licked her nose, I rubbed her face, I
nipped at her ear and purred louder and louder until
I knew I had won her over as well. The daughter
kept telling her, "Mom, you have to take this kitten,
this is the one, you just can't leave this little guy." I
was so happy when I heard this! I was finally going
to have a real home! At last I thought a place of
my own and parents all to myself. But then all of
a sudden I felt sad. The mother handed me back to
my keeper and said, "Let's just take a look around
and see some other kittens." I was put back into
my cage, my dreams shattered. With big sad eyes, I
watched them leave my room. I crawled to the back
of my cage, sad and all alone again.

Some time had passed, which to me felt like an
eternity. Then I heard their voices again. The same
two ladies were coming back to my cage. I was so
excited to see them! I prayed and prayed that they
were coming back to take me. As they came closer
and closer to my cage with big smiles on their faces,
I then realized they are. They are coming back to
take me! I was so thrilled! They took me out of my
cage again. Again, I turned on my cute charms, and
purred and purred and purred even louder this time.
And rubbed and rubbed and rubbed even harder. I

was so happy to see them! I thought to myself, "Are they really going to take me home this time?" I hope so. And then my prayers were answered; they are taking me. They are taking ME! I was then put back in my cage and they all went off to do some kind of paperwork. Shortly after, I was taken to the vet and given a complete overhaul and a good bill of health. My new family was coming back to get me later that afternoon and I couldn't wait. You see, they pushed to take me that day, you know, and I was so grateful and lucky because from what I understand, I wasn't at all what they were looking for.

First of all, they didn't want a male cat. They wanted a female, tabby or striped; preferably a Maine Coon. I was none of these. I was a male, dark grey, black and white. If I do say so myself, I think I'm pretty cute. One eye is black, the other white, I sometimes look cross-eyed, and I am mostly grey and black, with a patch of white here and there. I'm too cute for words, if you ask me. So basically, they didn't really choose me. I chose them and won them over with my adorableness.

Later that afternoon they came to take me home. I was all primped and proper and ready to go. I was now on my way to my new home. I was so excited I could hardly wait. I was not put in a cat carrier; I was carried out in the daughter's arms, and sat patiently and quietly on her lap until we arrived at my new home. I was to be a surprise for my new daddy. He didn't know anything about this and I couldn't wait to meet him!

When we arrived at my new home, the daughter carried me in quietly covered in her arms—my new daddy was sitting on the couch. He had no idea what was going on. Everyone was all smiles and laughing. Then he saw me peek out from under her arm. I was so tiny then and was easily hidden. He laughed and said "what is that—a kitten?" Then a huge smile appeared on his face as the daughter placed me in his arms. It was love at first sight. I could tell he was pleased. Once again, I turned on my powerful cute charms—this time to him. I purred my usual purrs, rubbed my usual rubs, licked and sniffed as before until I won him over with my charms and he accepted me. He was very happy, I could tell. He was all smiles!

After pleasing my new daddy, I then began to explore my new surroundings. I didn't know where to begin, I just went nuts! I had to explore every inch of my new home. I ran and ran, from room to room bumping into things, bouncing off walls, sliding on rugs and knocking things over. I was having the time of my life! I was free at last and had all this space to run around in! I couldn't have been any happier. And I know I brought such joy to them as well because they were all full of smiles and laughing at every silly little thing I did; which was basically going totally crazy. I loved my new surroundings. This was my home now. And I was so happy to be there.

I had a new family . . . I was home at last!

A Cat's Name...

What's In a Cat's Name?

Now it was time to find me a cute name.

They had plenty of time to observe my personality. Hmmm . . . . what would they call me, I thought? See, I told you earlier there was a story to my name. Just so you know, I am not an outdoors cat. So after a few days of them observing me that first weekend, and trying to figure out my adorable personality, they were all sitting on the back porch contemplating a name. I could only watch from behind a screened door because I was not allowed outside. I didn't mind. But I do know that I did not like being alone. So I sat patiently there behind the screened door until someone would join me inside.

That would usually be my daddy. You see, he would get bored so easily with woman-talk.

Names were going back and forth that day, until my mommy thought of a cute name that her mother used to call her brother. He was the only boy of seven children, mind you. She said to the daughter, "When your Uncle Marty came home from school, or wherever he was, my mother would say to him, 'here's my little Me'nino!' Italian slang which her mother might have made up, meaning "my little boy." How PERFECT! That settled it—they both agreed my name would officially be changed to Me'nino. My daddy liked it too. And I love it! I'm a true Me'nino through and through. Their "little boy."

So from that moment on, I became Me'nino. So it was finally settled. I had the cutest name ever because I'm the cutest kitten ever!

Later on my daddy shortened it, and would just call me Nino. I would only come to him when he called "Nino."

Others have tried to get me to come to them when they called me Nino, but I ignored them and went about my business. I'm stubborn that way.

Only my daddy can call me Nino.

My Cuteness . . .

My Cuteness Shines On!

I now have a cute name to go with my cute personality.

So once I became more and more comfortable in my new home, which took all of one day, I began to play and put on a show for my new parents. Remember, I'm only a kitten of four months or so, so I'm full of energy. So much so, that on my first day home, I just ran crazy. I wouldn't stop and couldn't stop playing. Not only did I play by myself to show off; I played with anyone who would play with me. I didn't stop until everyone went to bed. You would have thought I'd be exhausted after a day of no rest, and all play. But I wasn't, I was just so happy that I didn't want to waste one minute of valuable play and exploration time in my new surroundings. I finally settled down after everyone went to bed. Sort of; I still explored the house all alone, but was much quieter about it.

After my first weekend with them all, the daughter went back to her home. See, she usually only stayed three or four days at a time. I did miss her though because we had quality playtime. She made me chase things, and she would throw things up in the air so I could catch them and just run me crazy. Before she left, she showed me this huge stuffed cat that was always on the back of their couch. Well, I just went crazy over that thing. It was so real looking. First, I wasn't sure if it was alive or not and if I should defend my territory or what! So I would creep up to it and sniff at it and try to figure it out. Then I realized it was not moving or showing any signs of life when I did all this. So I would just attack it like it was alive using my natural predator instincts. I would grab it by the neck and straddle it, roll with it, bite it, and then just lick it. I loved licking things, all kinds of things, especially little furry things, even if they are fake tasting.

My family was always yelling at me to stop licking. Stop it! They yelled. But I didn't listen. I'm

I just kept on licking and licking
to me and made me stop by taking
me. The daughter would take that
away from me and throw it in different
s. That didn't stop me! I would just go fetch
d attack it and lick it again. This ritual was
epeated over and over again. We did this for hours
on end. After a while it became a game and it was
such great fun.

Finally, I was exhausted and just couldn't play
with it anymore. I fell fast asleep exhausted from
fighting and playing with it all day. I would snuggle
up to it and sleep with it until the daughter woke me
up to start playing all over again. But for now . . .

Me'nino needs his rest now! Good Night!

In the meantime, enjoy my photo album until
my next chapter begins.

My Photo
Album . . .

. . . It's all about ME . . .

. . . Me'nino Costello!

1st day in my new home!
Time to explore!

Playtime for "Nino"

Rest time for "Nino"

"Nino"

Don't I look like a "Nino?"

Me and my friend.

Time for bed everyone!

Waiting to play.

My little table by the window.

Waiting for my parents.

Mommy's lap all comfy cozy.

Daddy's computer desk.

I'm just too cute for words!
Got my daddy's foot!

Destruction taking place!
WHAT FUN!

This plant didn't stand a chance.

Santa & me!
Guess what I did with him . . .

I would SMACK him . . .

and SMACK him Again!

**One of my special sleeping /
hiding places!**

Just being cute as always . . .

PAWS!

Show me your PAWS!

My messy litter box.
Can you find my bottle caps?

Who's a handsome boy . . .

. . . Me'nino is!
That's who!

Me and Mommy August 2011

Me and Daddy Today 2012

Loving Parents . . .

My Loving Parents...

After the daughter went home, I had my parents all to myself. I would entertain them for hours on end, days upon days, weeks, upon weeks, and months upon months. They loved me, and I loved them back. I brought them such joy, that the stress of mommy's illness was lessened. There was happy laughter all the time and mommy would tell people about all the silly things I did. It was wonderful. I was so happy that I made her happy. But I bonded more with my daddy because I knew he would need me most. Plus, he was the only one that was allowed to feed me, take care of me, and clean my litter box. And I pity my daddy; FOR I CAN CLEAR A ROOM after I use my litter box! And I have, many times. Don't know—must be the stuff they put in my cat food. P—ew! For a tiny little kitty, daddy would always say I pooped like a horse.

I was truly enjoying my new home. I was never happier, and I know my parents were enjoying me too. We had this one game we played every night. I knew when they were getting ready to go to bed, so I would race them to their bedroom and jump under the sheets and wait for them to come and find me. Then they would rough me up with the sheets. That was such fun. Then I would cuddle up between them and go to sleep. We did this every night. I usually didn't sleep through the night though. I would get up and want to be fed. I love to eat. And like I said earlier, that was my daddy's job. So up he'd get and off we'd go to the kitchen and I would be fed.

During one of my many explorations, I remember there was this one thing in their bedroom that did frighten me—this shinny thing. It terrified me! The first time I walked by it, I saw another CAT! And I did not like that! This is my house, and I will fight to the end to defend it. So I tried and tried, but for some reason, this cat was not fighting me back. I would scratch it, smell it, punch it, and look behind it, but there was nothing there. So then I just ignored it and went about my business. That was the last time I fought with that funny creature they call a mirror.

The days were about the same, lots of play, lots of company and lots of joy. I like people and I don't like to be left alone. When mommy and daddy would go off and do whatever they needed to do outside the house; I would run to my little table by the window and watch them leave. Then I would go off and take a nap and wait for them to return. When they did return, I would know and would run back to that little table and watch them come in. Then I would race to the front door to greet them in hopes of getting some playtime; which I would usually get plenty of.

I would spend lots of time sleeping on mommy's lap during the day and spend hours sitting with daddy while he used his computer at night. I was a very happy little kitty, and special too. Mommy and daddy often called me their "little angel without wings".

Monthly Play Dates . . .

The Daughter's Monthly Play Dates...

When the daughter returned on her monthly visits, she would always bring me treats and toys. On one of her visits, she brought me this one toy I especially loved! It was a stuffed Clouded Leopard in a lying down position. Not much bigger than me and I loved that thing. It was the perfect size, and like the stuffed cat before, I would do the same things with it, only I could carry this one around with me in my teeth, like freshly killed prey. They would tease me by taking it away from me and throwing it in different locations just like before. And I would do the same thing with this one. Attacking and licking it. I had lots of fun with that Clouded Leopard. And they loved watching me play with it. It also had little beads in the paws that made a noise when the daughter banged it on her lap. No matter what room I was in, I would hear that funny little noise and I would come running from wherever I was. As soon as I saw it in her hands, I would speak and she would throw it to the floor so I could attack it just like before.

Yep, you heard right, I speak and I am a little chatter box too. Whenever they wanted to get my attention with one of those stuffed toys, or anything for that matter, all they had to do was throw it, and before it landed I would let out a "plluuerrt mew" kind of sound and run after whatever they threw. It's just a little warning sound that says "I'm coming!" Then I would pounce on it.

My daddy started to make me ask for my dinner too since he now knew I could talk. When he would get ready to feed me, he would ask me, "Nino, tell me what you want?" and I would have to answer him with that same kind of "plluuerrt mew". He would laugh and then he would feed me. I became very spoiled that way, for I too learned that if I talked to him, he would give me treats. I especially LOVE treats. And then I learned very quickly to use my little chatter to get pretty much whatever I wanted whether it was treats, dinner, toys or just attention, all I had to do was "plluuerrt mew."

There was this one weekend when the daughter was visiting that made me very confused. I remember it all too well because I was so sad and traumatized from the whole incident. That was the day I thought they were getting rid of me. For some reason, they packed me up in my carrier and took me out of the house. MY HOUSE! Where are they taking me I thought? I ended up back at that shelter! NO! I DON'T WANT TO COME BACK HERE! I knew this because I recognized the smells. I thought to myself, what did I do wrong? Do you not love me anymore? Why don't you want me? They put me on the counter and then some stranger came over to me and was looking at my eyes and poking at me and making me feel very uncomfortable. There was a lot of talk going on, and then we left.

We returned home but I wasn't sure if I was staying or not. So I got very depressed and hid. I didn't want to leave my home so I wasn't letting them get anywhere near me. After some time, I felt comfortable again and I came out of hiding and started to play. I trusted them now and then realized they weren't getting rid of me; they would never get rid of me. I just had some kind of eye problem, "eye snot" the doctor called it. They were just getting me checked out. Thank goodness! I was so scared they didn't want me anymore and I certainly didn't want to leave them. I loved them very much and was having way too much fun with my new family.

Lots of fun! The daughter taught me how to fetch with small plastic bottle caps. Boy, those were such fun toys. She would scratch the sides of it until I came in the room and then she would toss them at me.

Of course you know I always spoke before it hit the floor. That's why she did it, to make me speak so she could hear my cute chatter. The scratching noise would drive me nuts and get my attention wherever I was. I would hear that nose and I would come running and chatter up my usual chatter and then fetch those bottle caps. I would carry them all over the place, and swat them around the hardwood floors and chase after them. They slid so nicely on hardwood floors. I especially loved lifting the edges of rugs and hiding the caps underneath and then try to get them out. I could spend hours doing that. I would also carry them to my water bowl and drop them in and try to fish them out of the water. Many times I tipped over that water bowl and got my daddy mad. I would also play with them around my litter box, but that wasn't nice. I would be half in and out of my litter box and try to pick the cap up off the floor and put it in the litter. That was dirty stuff so I eventually stopped doing that and just played with them under rugs and by my water bowl. I know I must have lost lots of them because they all disappeared. I think there might be at least one hundred under their couch.

My daddy and I would also play together on the floor a lot. He would make me fight with him. He would pull his sleeves down to protect his hands, because I did have razor sharp claws and would scratch him by mistake. I don't mean to, it's just I'm still a little kitten and in time will learn not to scratch. Anyway, he would get down on all fours at my level and bat at me to get me to fight him, which I did.

Then after we were done playing around, so he thought, he would get up and start walking away. Little did he know I was not done playing! I would ambush him and ATTACK him from behind. I would grab at his legs and feet and chase him around, trying to bite at his legs and feet. Then he would laugh and pick me up and hold me up under the arms and shake me a little for fun. I didn't like that so much, so I would try and scare him by spreading out my PAWS and CLAWS wide!!! Like I was going to swat him in the face. I would try, but I would never actually hit him. This was just a fun thing we did to each other. Sometimes he would just pick me up that way so I would show him my PAWS. The daughter loved the PAWS. She would always tell my daddy to make me do the PAWS by saying "PAWS! Show me your PAWS!" It became a cute thing we did after a while.

The other things I liked to play with were plants! Plants were FUN! They had this one plant on their dining room table that I loved and it was always getting me into trouble. They would yell at me, and try to make me stop playing with it. But being my usual stubborn self, I just ignored them and would go back to playing with the plant. There was just something about it that made it fun to play with. It had stringy things sticking out all over that I loved to chew and play with, or maybe it was just the dirt. I liked the smell of dirt. Whatever the reason, I did have a lot of fun tearing that plant apart. My parents eventually gave in, and let me play with it. Then after I completely destroyed this plant, they got rid of it. I would find other flowers and plants, or whatever they put on the dining room table to play with. Nothing was safe if left on that table. I really really liked the dining room table.

I remember one fall day there was all this little white fluffy stuff falling from the sky. I watched it from my little table at the front window. This was interesting stuff. I wanted to play and catch this stuff. The daughter was still visiting at this time and she took me outside. BURR it was cold. Remember, I am not an outdoors kind of kitty. She made me touch that white stuff with my paws. All it did was make me shake my paws wildly trying to get that stuff off. It made my tootsies all cold and wet. I did not like that stuff. Nothing was extra special about this white fluffy stuff to give me any reason to play with it now. I lost interest fast. I liked by toys better, so I would just go back to my box of toys and try to find something interesting to play with.

I do have my very own special toy box. It was a shoe box I loved to play in and sleep in. Again, the perfect size for me. I was still kind of small. I would play with my toys inside it, around it, on top of it, and through the little holes the box had. I did amuse myself well. It certainly didn't take much to keep me occupied. Especially during my first Christmas.

My first Christmas was a happy time for me. For I loved that Christmas tree! It was full of all these nice shiny things, which moved when you touched them. They called them ornaments. I would play with all those ornaments and knock them down and bat them all over the house. I did on occasion break a few, but mommy only put the ones she wasn't that fond of on the bottom of the tree for me to play with. But I never did climb that tree. I did like it though; I liked the smell and I liked sleeping behind and under it. It was the closest thing to being outside as I would get.

There was also a cute Santa I would play with. He would tell me a story and bounce all around, THEN . . . with all his bouncing; I'd get frisky and just attack him, and attack him again until I wore myself out and feel asleep.

This was a very special time with my family; this one Christmastime.

Something is
Wrong...

Something is Terribly Wrong...

Things started to change after my first Christmas; I could feel a tension in my new home. My mommy wasn't her usual self and I could see she tired easily. I spent many hours sleeping with her on her lap. I still tried to be my frisky playful self, because I knew that would make her happy and smile. My daddy went back to work during this time, so it was just me and mommy most of the day. I would sit with her and lie with her and keep her company until daddy came home. We went about our usual business trying to keep joy in the house.

The daughter still came up for her monthly visit that winter but this one time she didn't leave. See, she usually only came for a few days at a time. I did have quality playtime but I could still sense there was something different in the way everyone was acting.

We still had some happy times. I remember something very funny that happened. I was playing in the basement one day, and when I came up (you see, the door was always left open so I could come and go as I pleased—I am spoiled!), I was TERRIFIED of what I saw. I wasn't sure if it was my mommy or some kind of creature. It was sitting in my mommy's spot on the couch. It was a weird looking thing, with a pointed head sticking up four inches high with a round thing on the top, and two stringy things going down either side of the pointed head. So, in my defense, I arched my back! My fur puffed up, and I went at it sideways for the kill. Then this funny looking thing started to laugh and called for the daughter to come quick. Then I realized it was my mommy! The daughter came in, and got hysterical when she saw how I was acting. Then I realized everything was okay and I relaxed. Come to find out, mommy was just cold so she had this funny looking hat on. Thank goodness it wasn't really a creature or I would have had to fight with it! Everyone did have a good laugh over that incident.

We were still trying to make special times together the best we could.

My mommy was becoming more and more tired each day. My daddy was more agitated and sad and the daughter was very very sad. She barely played with me anymore. Even I was becoming more and more sad. I did not really want to play. I started just lying around the house. I wasn't quite sure what was happening.

All I know is my mommy left the house one day that winter and didn't return.

Life Without Mommy . . .

Life Without My Mommy . . .

It's been some time since then. It's now just daddy and me. I know a part of my mommy is still within me and that part of me is the special part. Ever since our first meeting I knew she had a task in mind for me. When I chose her and she took me, I now know that it was to take care of my daddy when she left us. I am doing my part to honor her wishes by being my adorable self. I miss my mommy terribly, but daddy and I are doing okay; it will take some time. I try to ease his loneliness and pain and try to make him laugh. We are a special pair now, my daddy and me, and have a long journey ahead. I know my mommy is watching over us and we will never forget her.

Daddy and I have new special times now. We still get lots of company and I still show off my cute charms as much as I can. I see the daughter from time to time and she still runs me ragged. She also brings me special treats. Mommy would be proud of us for we are trying to go on living as she would want us to live. I will take good care of my daddy, for he needs me the most. I will make him happy, make him smile and make him laugh again.

For this is my story . . . . my promise to mommy.

Epilogue

I lost my beloved mother, Louisa, on February 1, 2012 to Lung Cancer.

It's now been over a year since my mother and I adopted this wonderful little kitten for my father. Me'nino has given him such joy and comfort words just can't describe. They are adorable together. One is more stubborn than the other. They test each other's patience on a daily basis. They are truly perfect for each other.

Me'nino has grown into a huge beautiful cat. He is more feisty and special than ever. He no longer cares for my visits like he used to as a kitten. He will play, but his focus is all on his daddy now; as it should be. He is definitely daddy's "little boy".

My mother continues to watch over us through this special kitty, now an adult cat. She is definitely a part of Me'nino. Precious Me'nino is her special gift to all of us.

She is always with us and always will be. Rest in peace mom—you are missed and loved.

ॐ ॐ

I hope this story provides some laughter and comfort for all those dealing with, or dealt with, a terrible disease. We had a long struggle, dad and me, and through the gift of just one special little kitten, we found such joy and happiness in the way this kitten pulled us through a really tough time.

He truly is our "little angel without wings."

This book is for you mom!

Acknowledgements

I thank my mother, Louisa, for who this story is about. For all the love and kindness she always showed me which inspired me to write this book for her. She was a very special lady to us and everyone she touched throughout her shortened life. She was always strong and positive throughout her illness which made it easier for my father and me to be strong and positive for her.

My father, Ronald, for all the love and kindness he gave me while growing up and the love and support he gave my mother during her illness and the 55 years they were together. His positive attitude throughout her illness helped me keep positive as well.

My husband, David, for the love, support and understanding he has given me throughout my mother's illness.

My dear friend Holly Zyara, through her experience and knowledge, spent endless hours helping me get through this difficult time.

The Ulster County ASPCA for which "Me'nino's Tail" might not have been written if it wasn't for the wonderful job they did in raising this adorable kitten and for the love and care they provide for all homeless and abused animals.